ANDREA SHELLEY

NEWMAN SPRINGS PUBLISHING
320 Broad Street
Red Bank, NJ 07701

First originally published by Newman Springs Publishing 2024

ISBN 979-8-89061-036-2 (Paperback)
ISBN 979-8-89061-037-9 (Digital)

Printed in the United States of America

For Megan who has always believed in me,
and Ali and Carter who inspire me every day

The morning school started, Moose took a look,
Inside my animal coloring book

"I can't go like this! I look like a coot!
And the animals here are much, much too cute!

I wish I were a kitten, sweet
and soft and small.
Who wants to pet a moose?
Who wants a moose at all?

I wish I were a pony! Kids
love to ride on those,

Or a little fluffy dog, dressed up in cozy clothes."
"Oh, come on, Moose, please don't be mean!
You're the best you that I've ever seen!"

"I wish I were a bear."
"A bear?"
"They don't tromp and tumble everywhere!
Their legs aren't tall and skinny things,
And best of all, they sleep till spring!"

"Oh, come on, Moose, please don't be mean!
You're the best you, that I've ever seen!"

"But I don't *want* to be a moose!"

He wailed.

6

"My feet are big, my rump is tailed!
I don't feel cool, I look so weird!

What kind of animal has a beard?
No. I don't want to be a moose."

He said.

"These antlers are heavy way up on my head.

I think I'll be a unicorn!
They're cute and sweet, and have *one* horn."

"But..."

"At last, I've found what I should be!
For people to like—no, love—clumsy me.
Just picture their faces!
When we get to school...

Wh–what are you wearing?"
"I think moose are cool."

"WHAT?!"

"I wish I had legs, knobby and tall,
I'd reach every shelf and catch every ball
I'd love more hair, I don't think that it's weird,
The king of the jungle has one awesome beard.

And as for the antlers, I want those as well!
No one else would have that show and tell.
What's wrong with your feet?
They're bigger than mine,
You run so fast, while I fall behind.
Yes, now you know, I can't help that it's true,
I wish I were as cool an animal as you."

"No!
Oh, my friend, please don't be mean!
You're the best you, that I've ever seen!
You're entirely good, I love you, you see,
You're my best friend, you're perfect to me."

"You're my best friend too, I love you as you are,
Let's be ourselves, that's got us one friend so far."

SCHOOL